I0491891

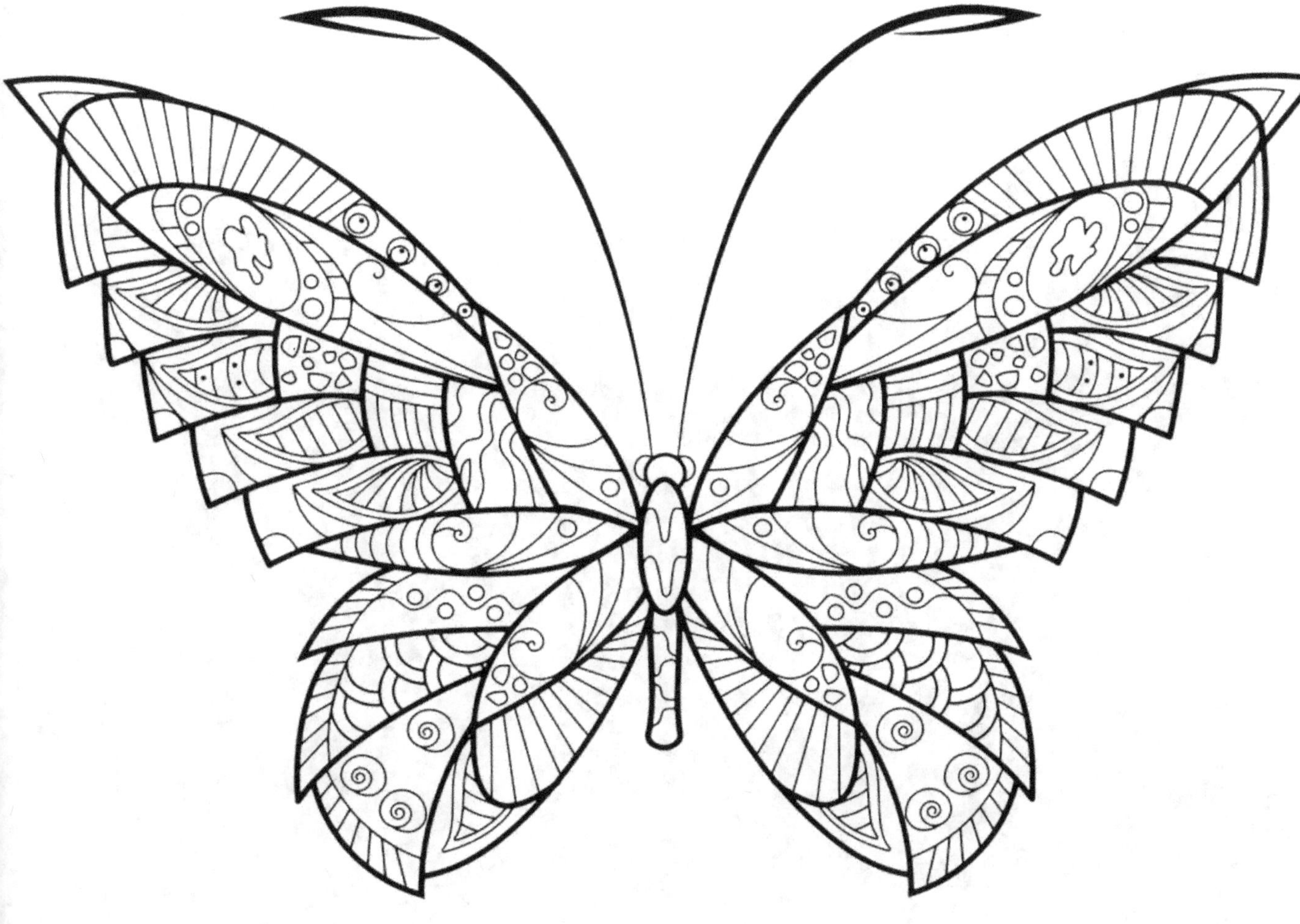

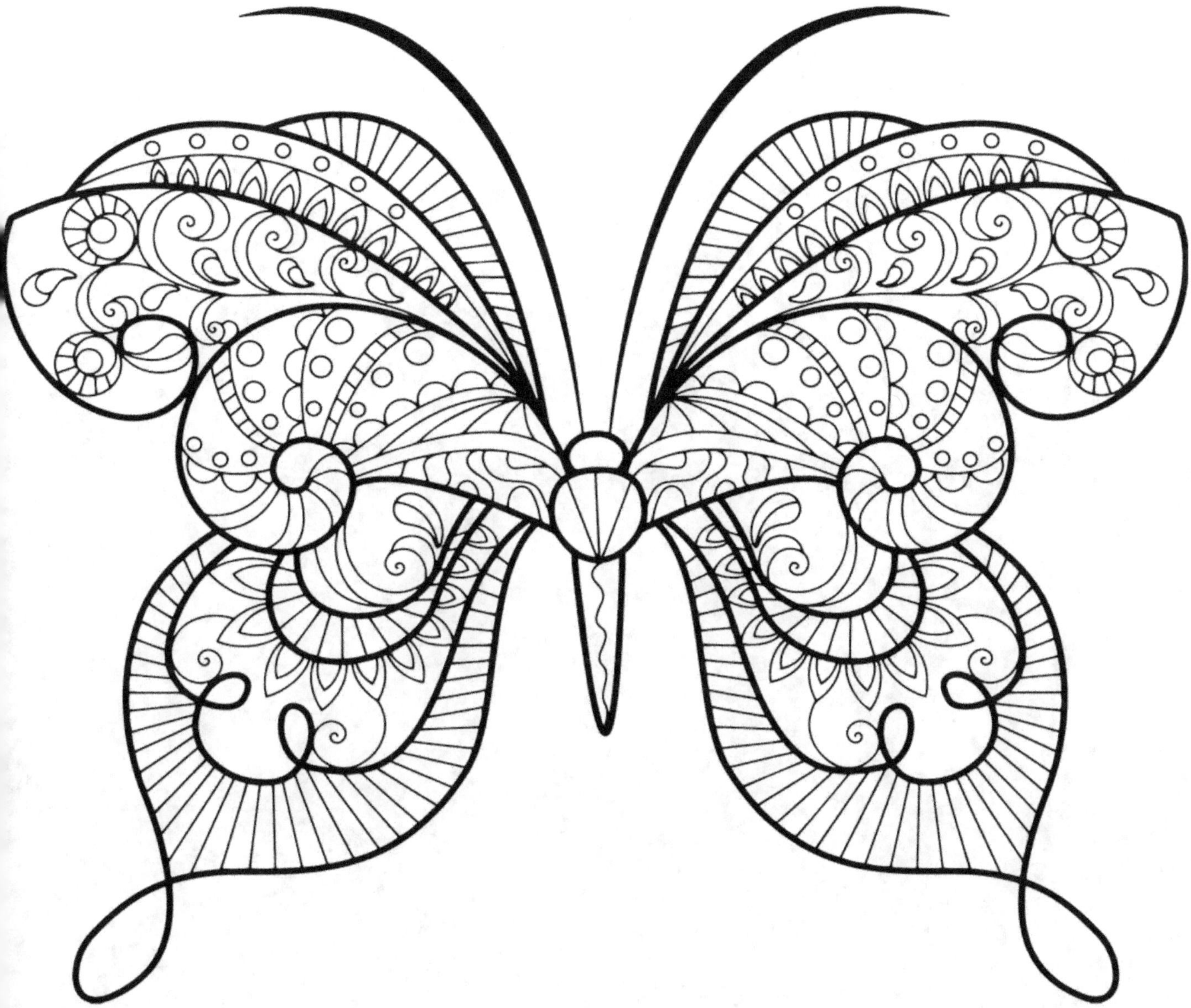

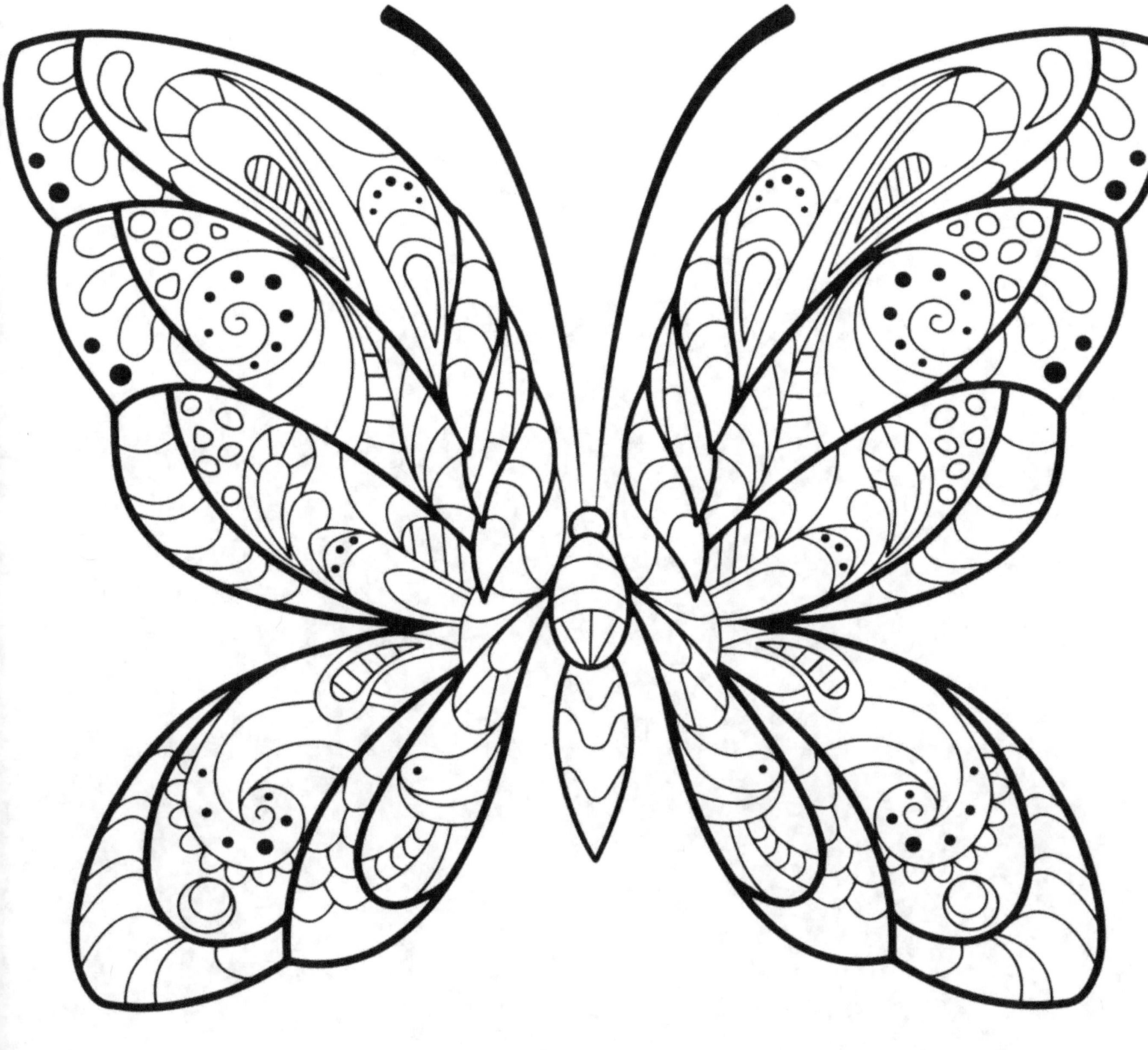

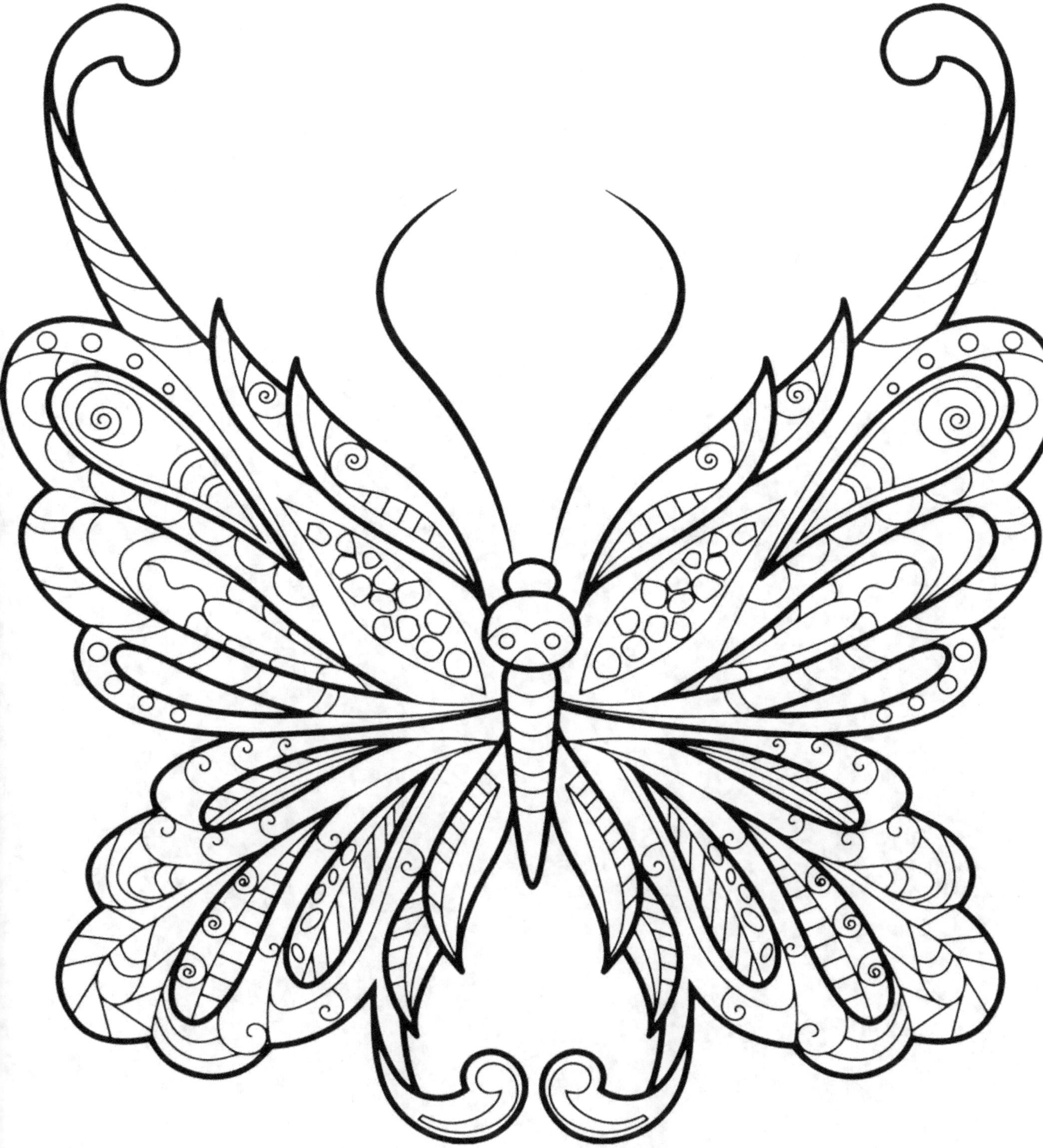

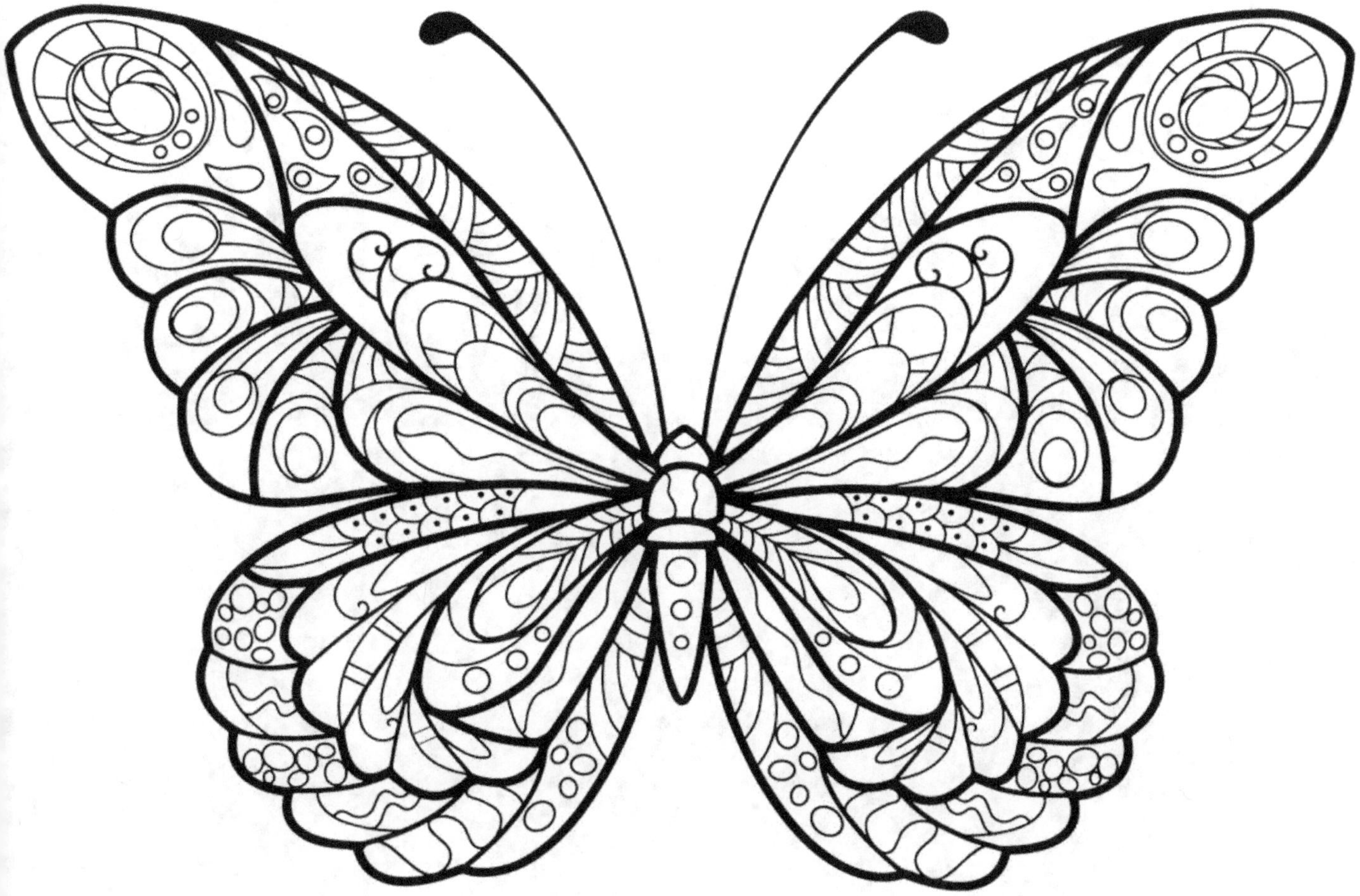

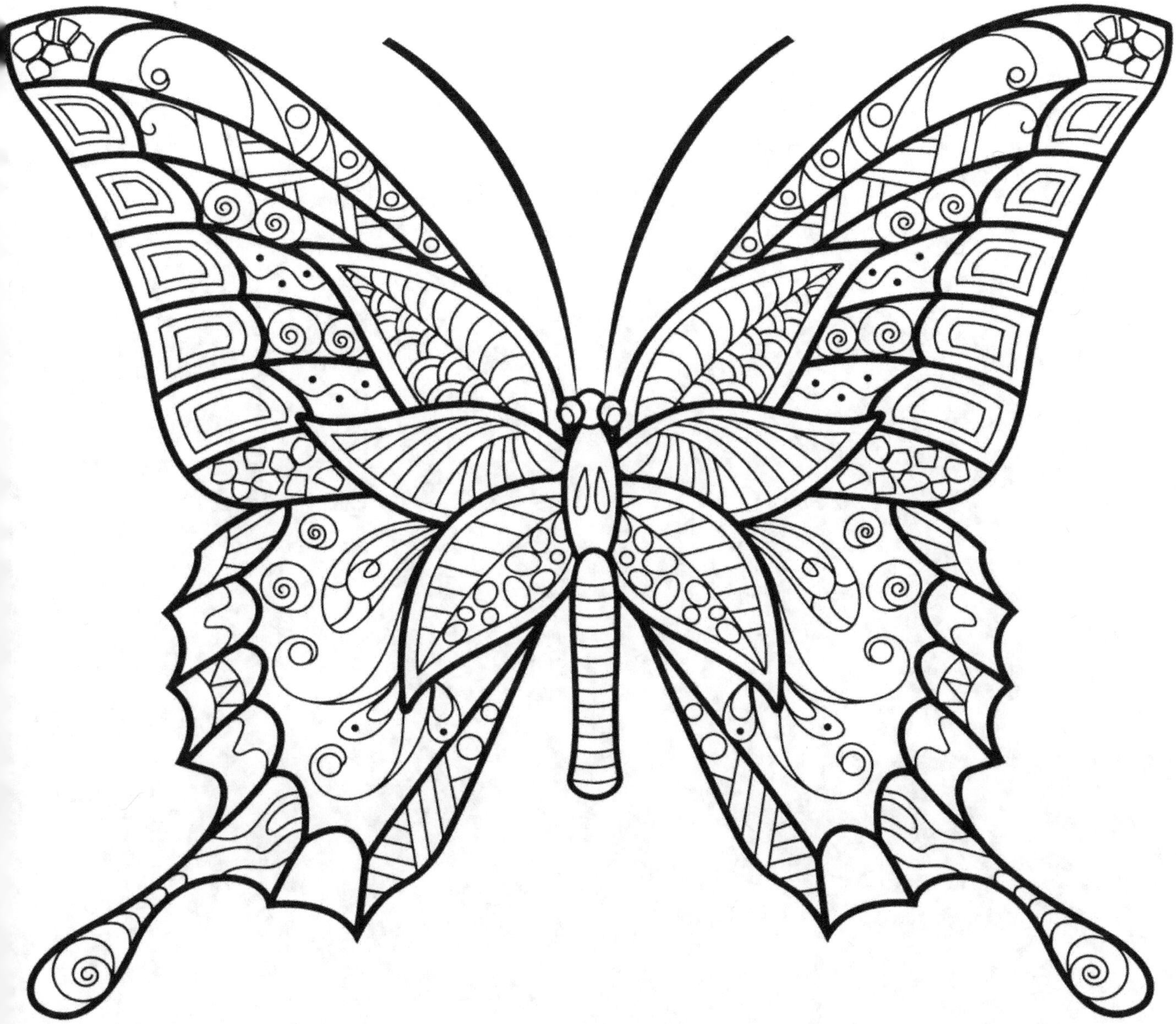

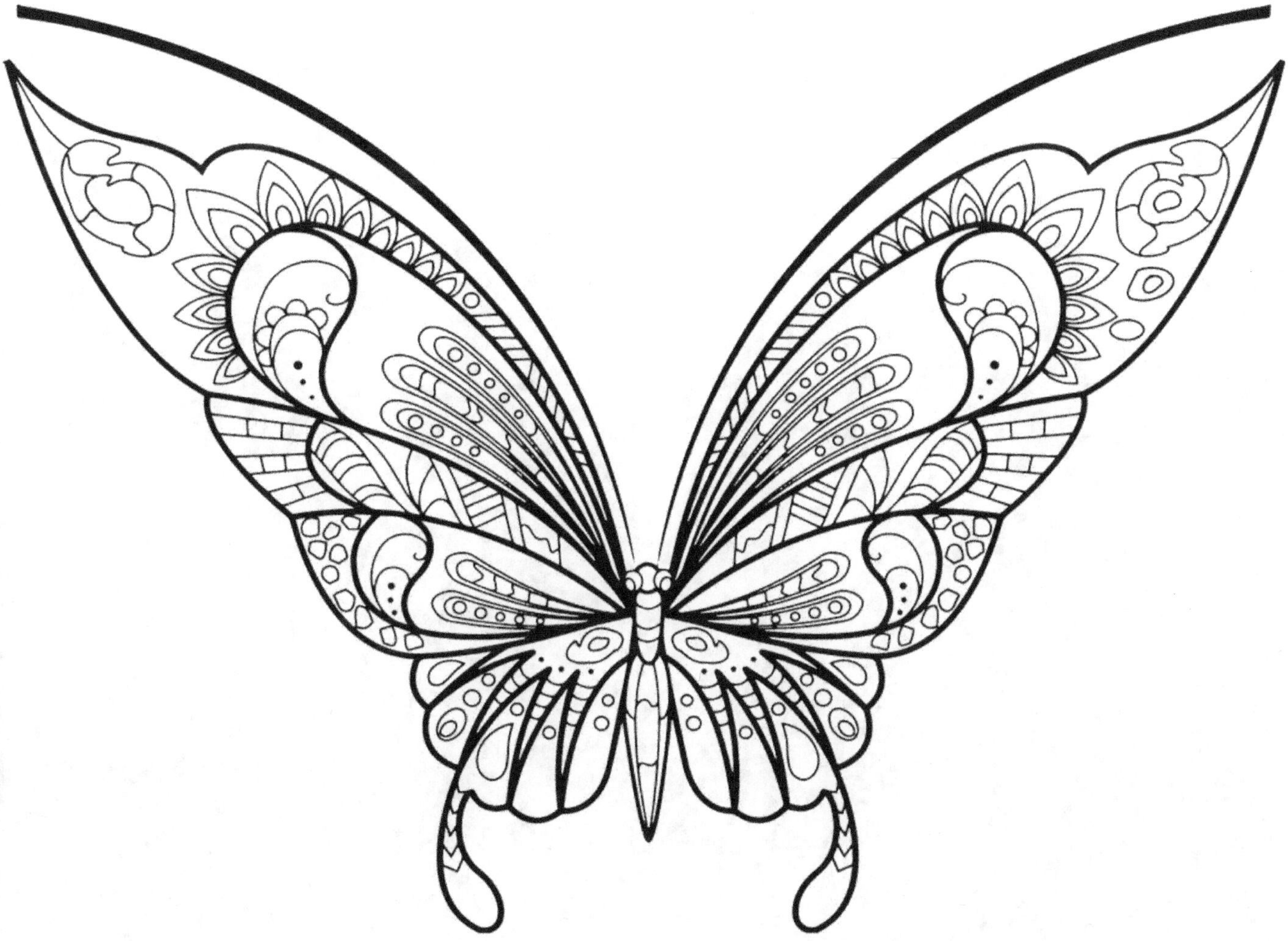

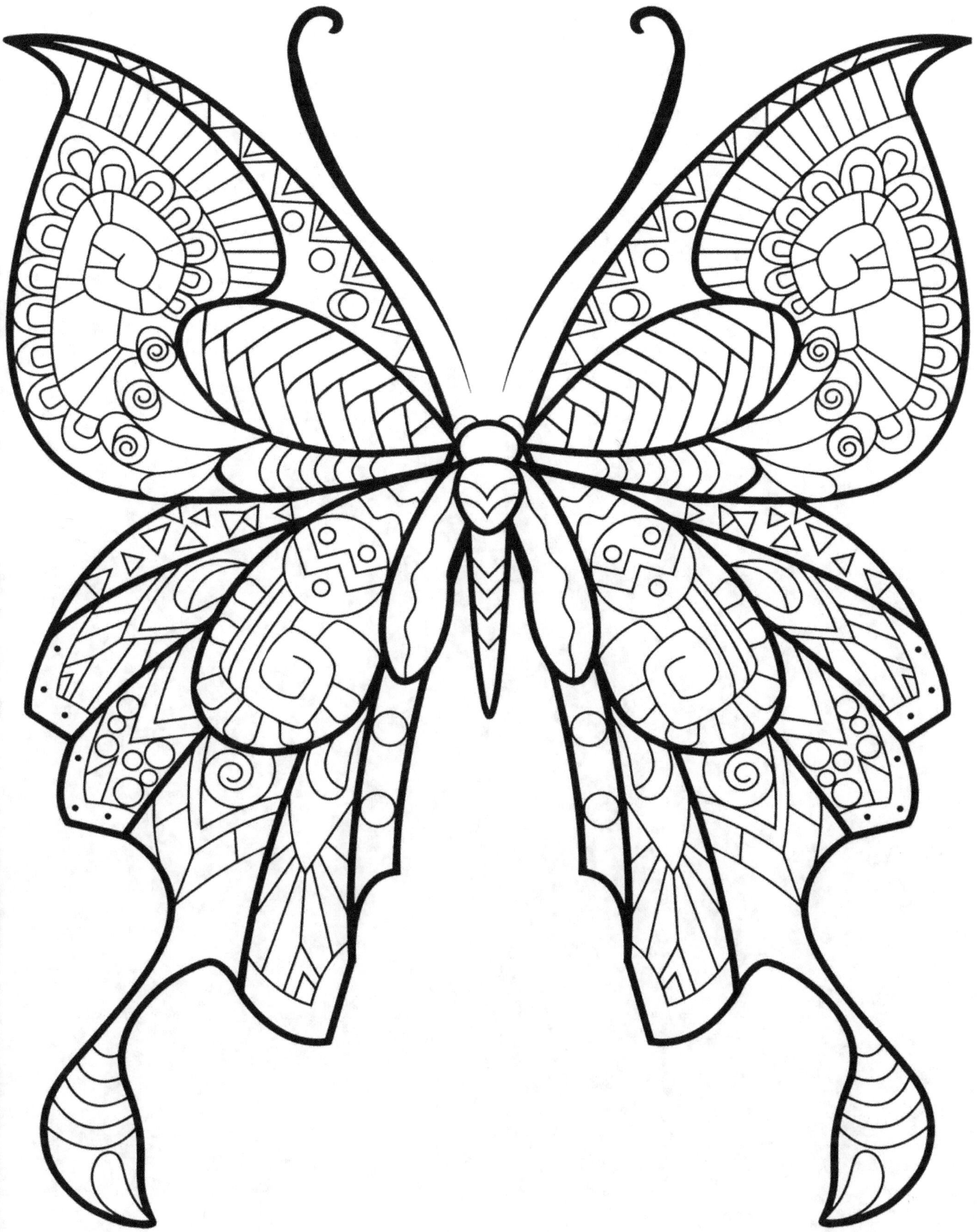

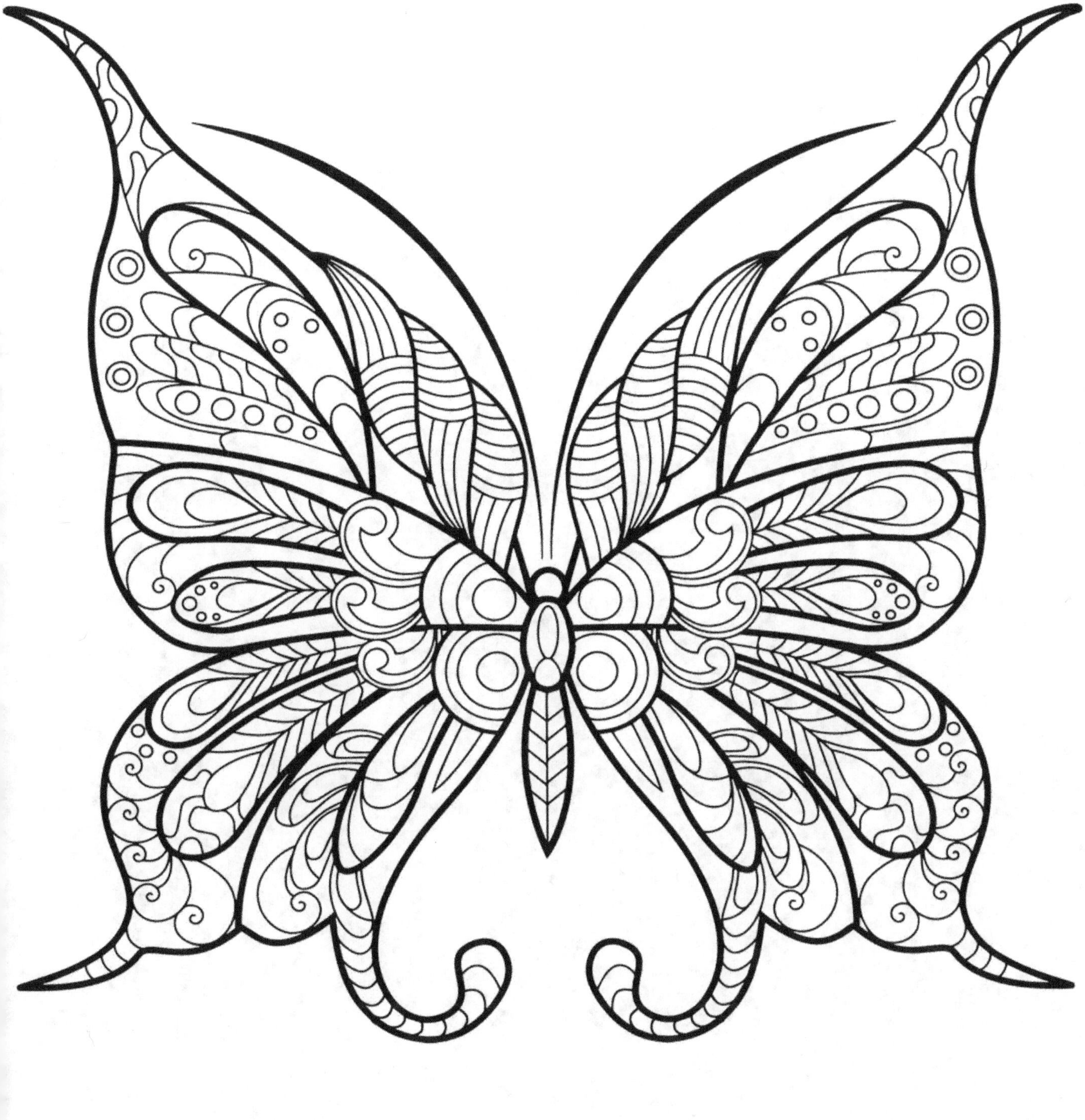

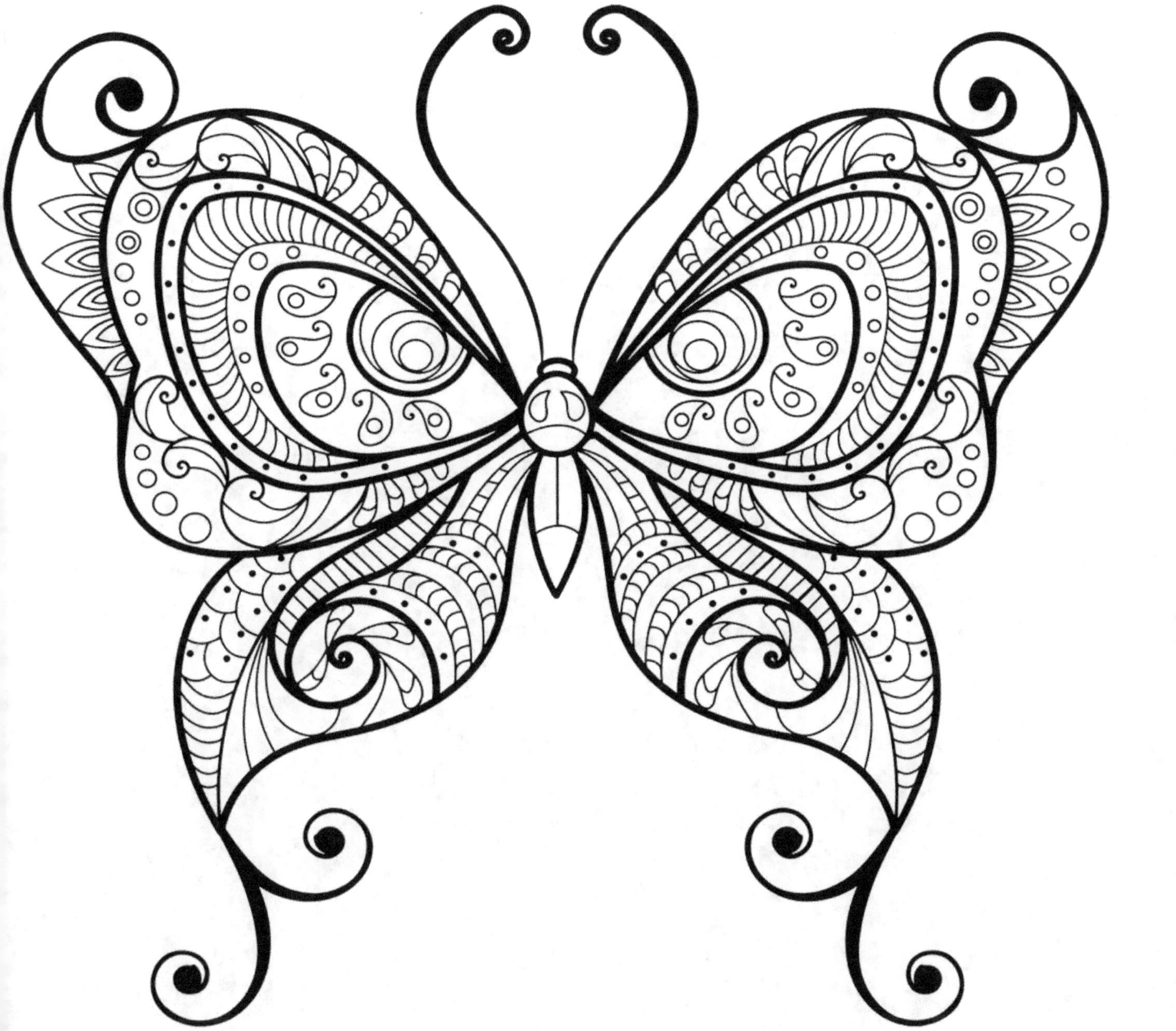

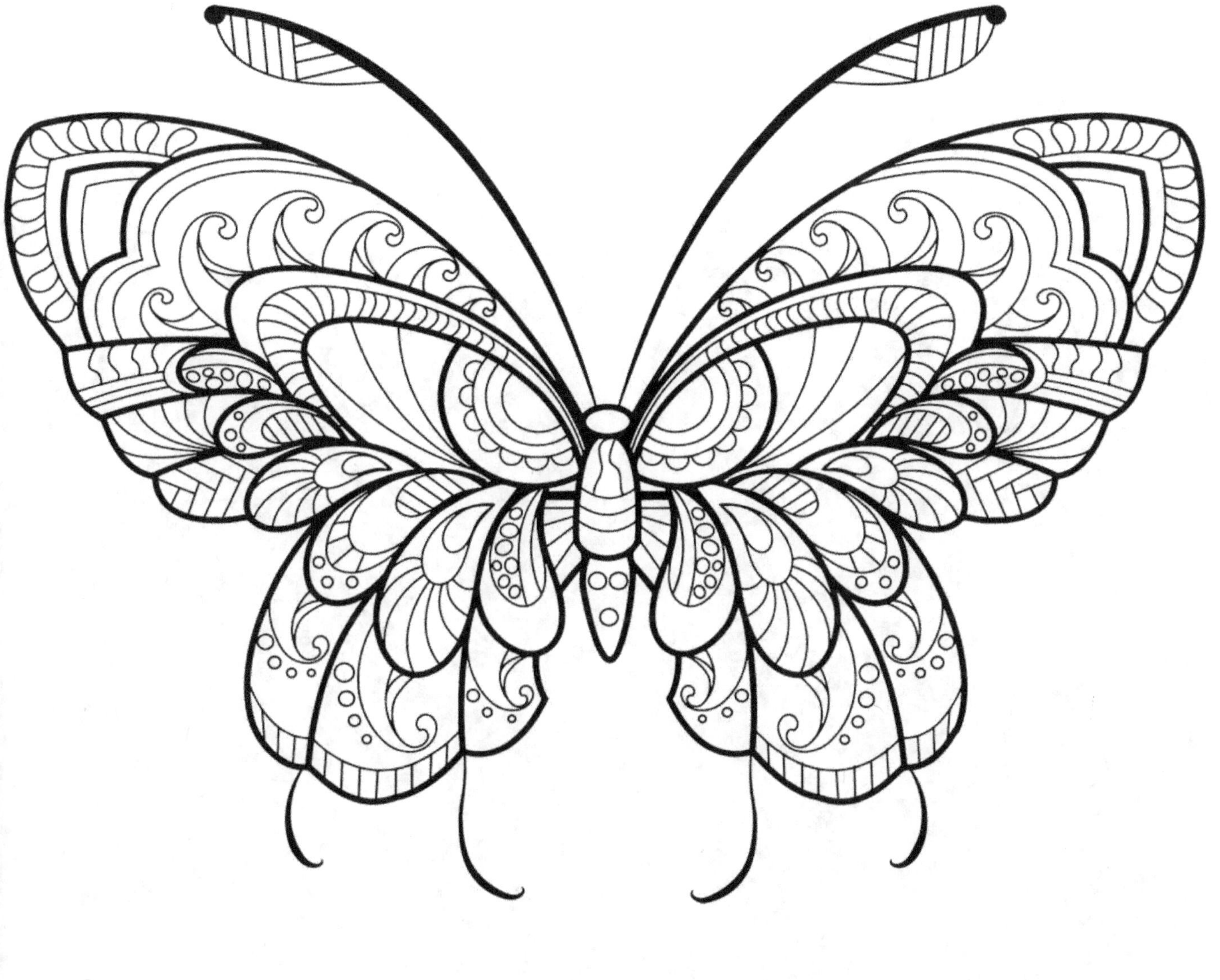

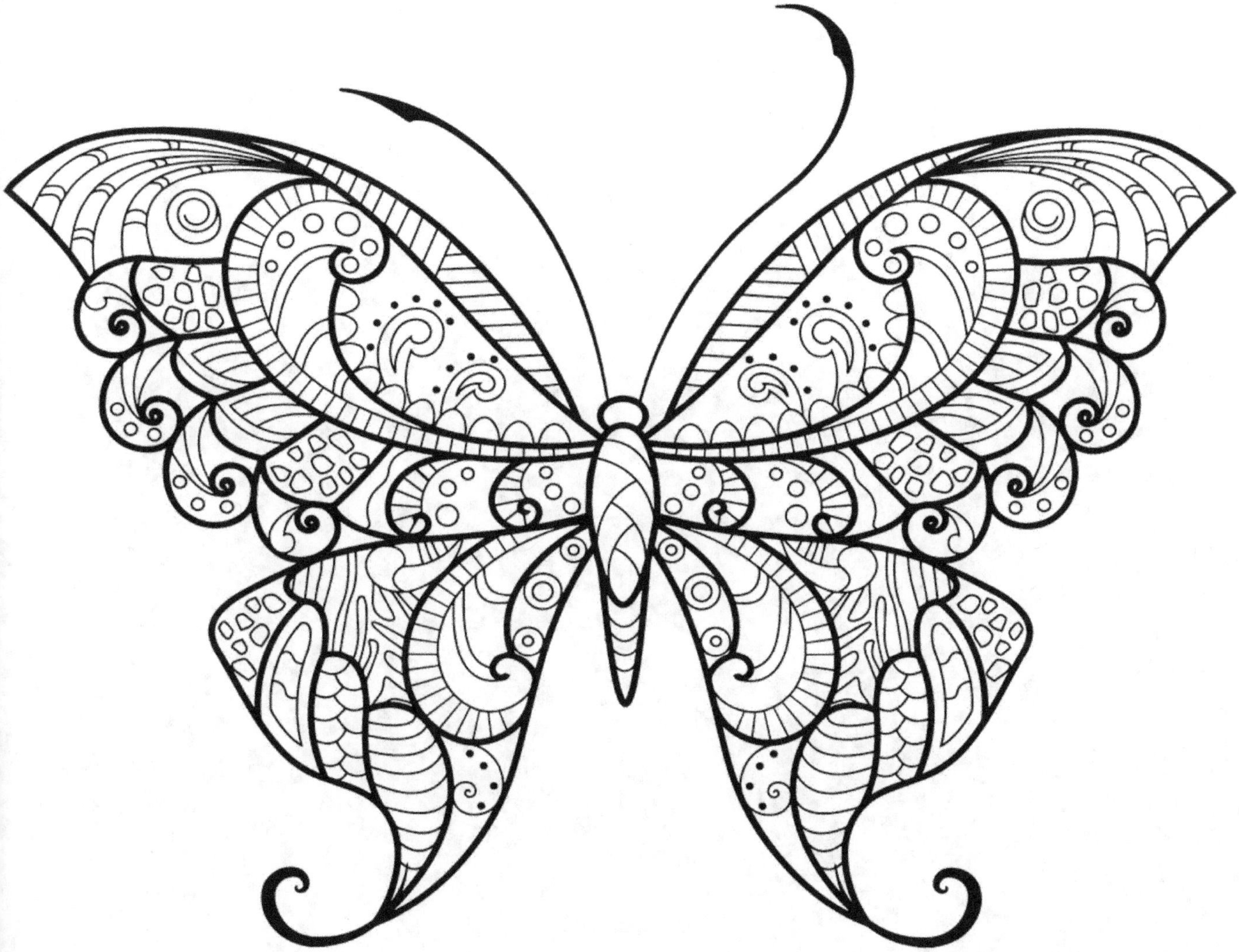

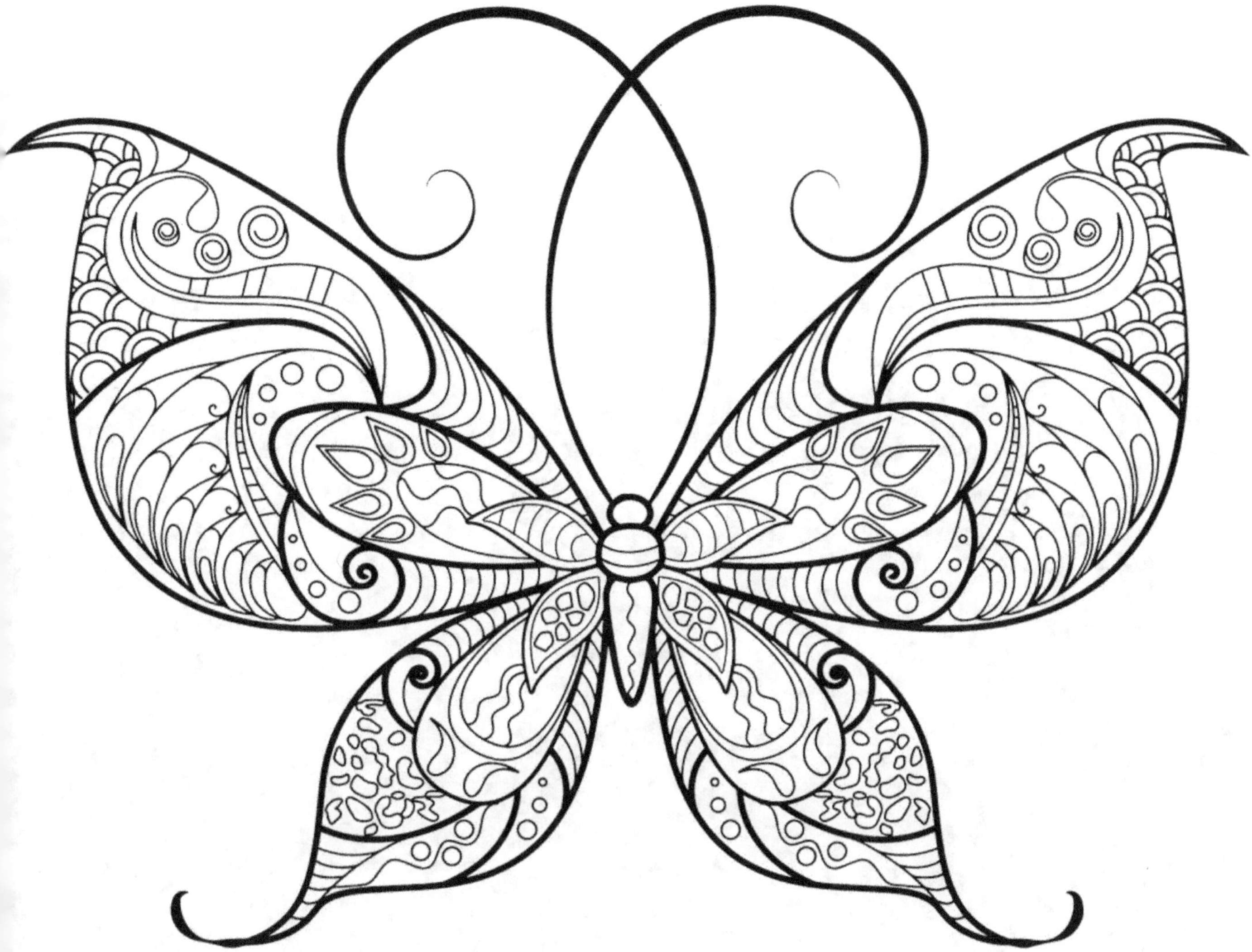

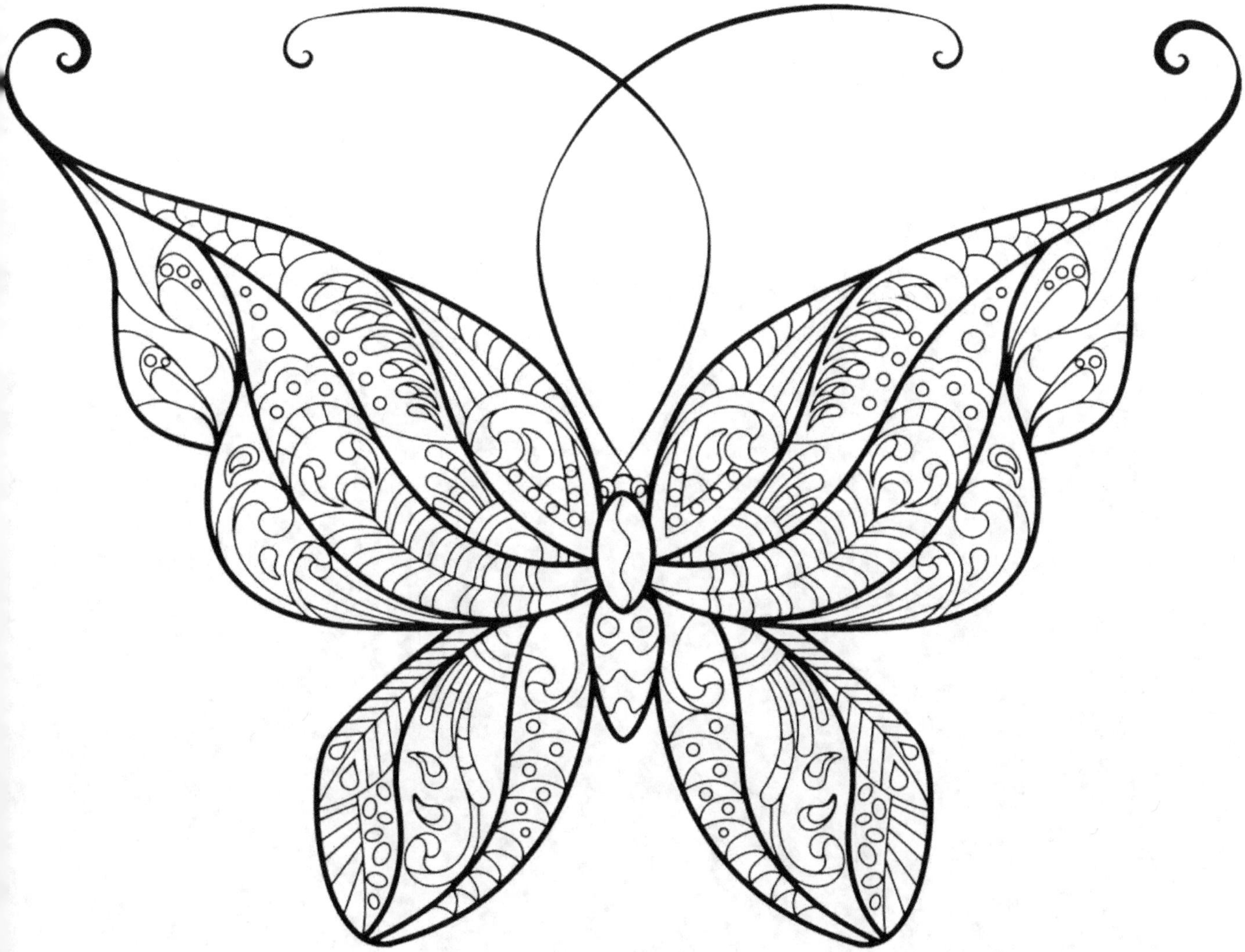

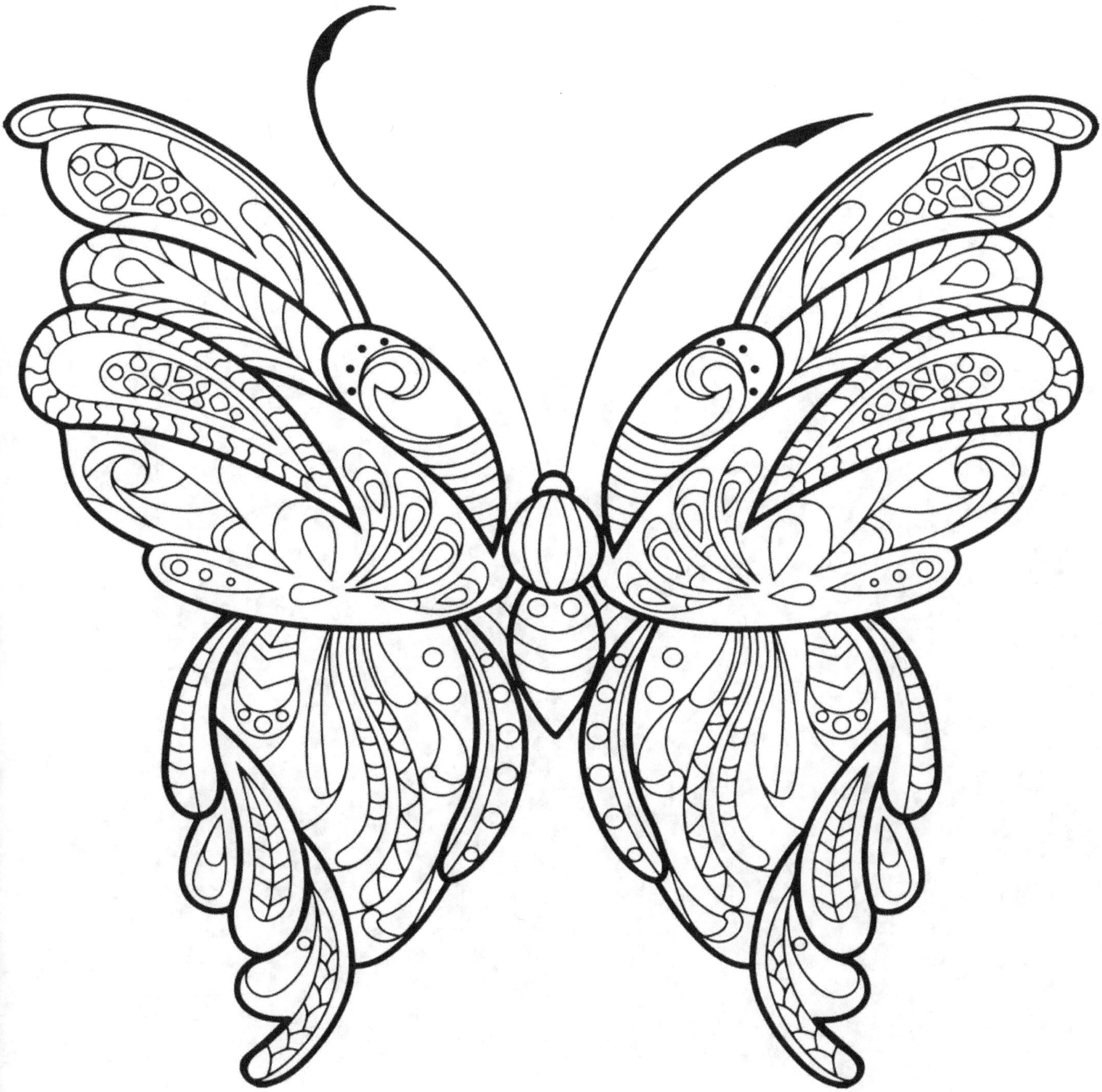

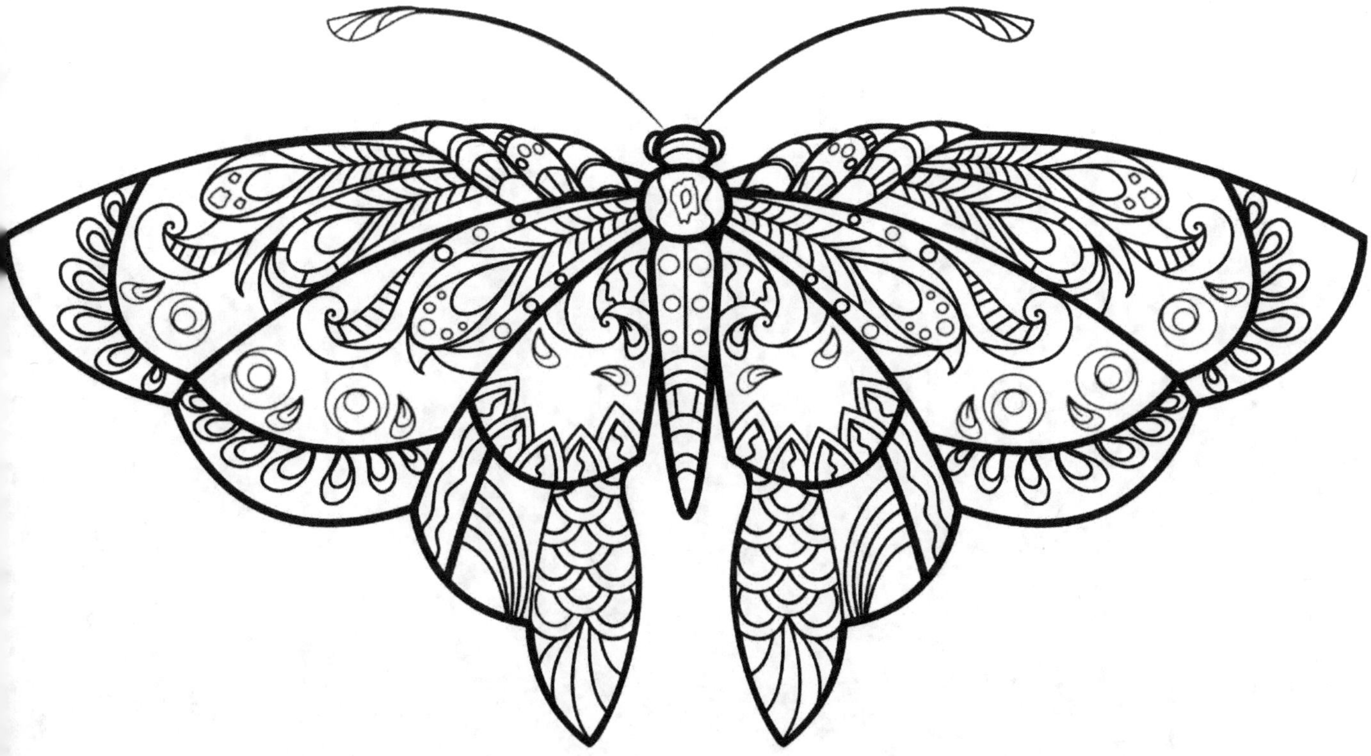

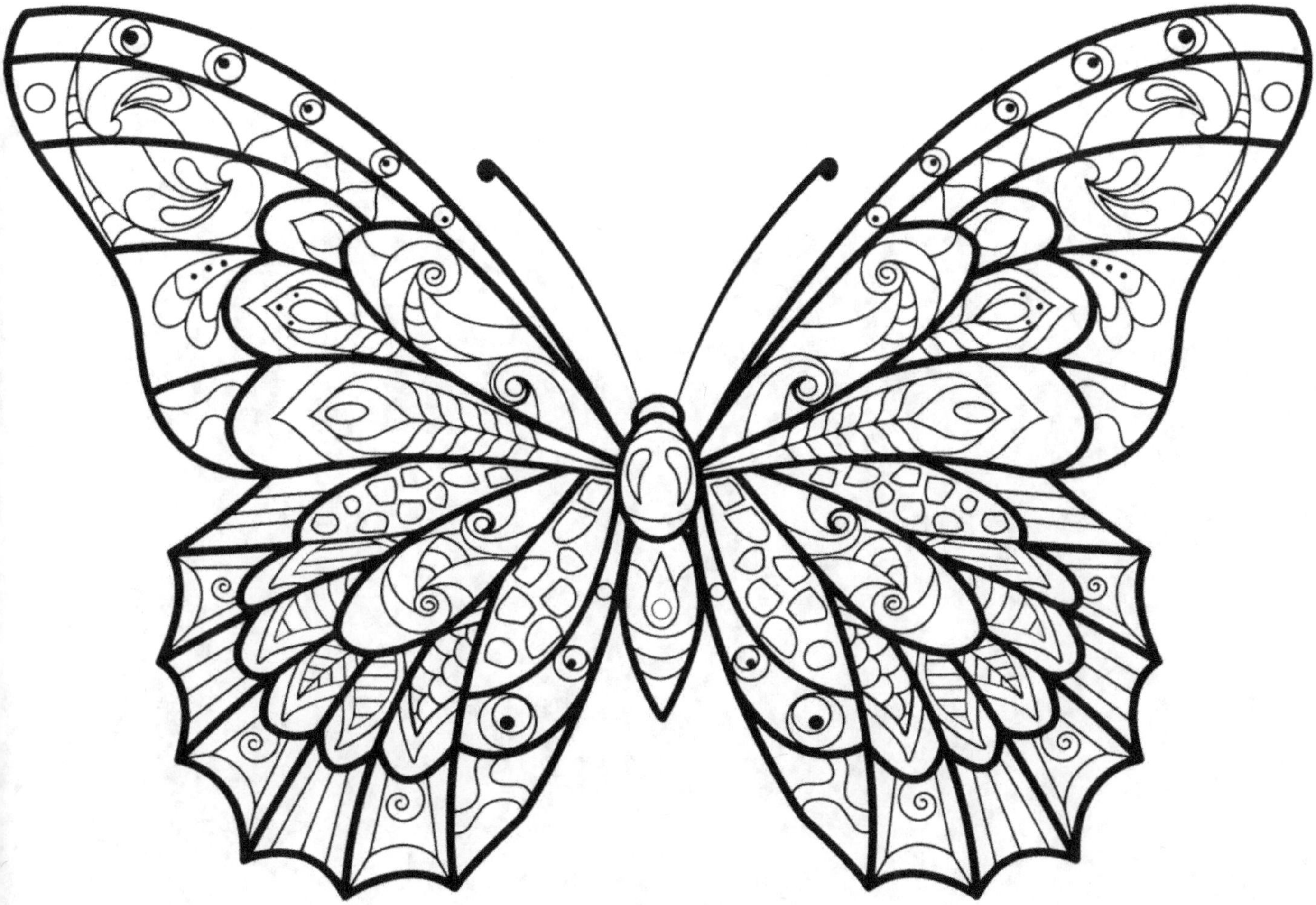

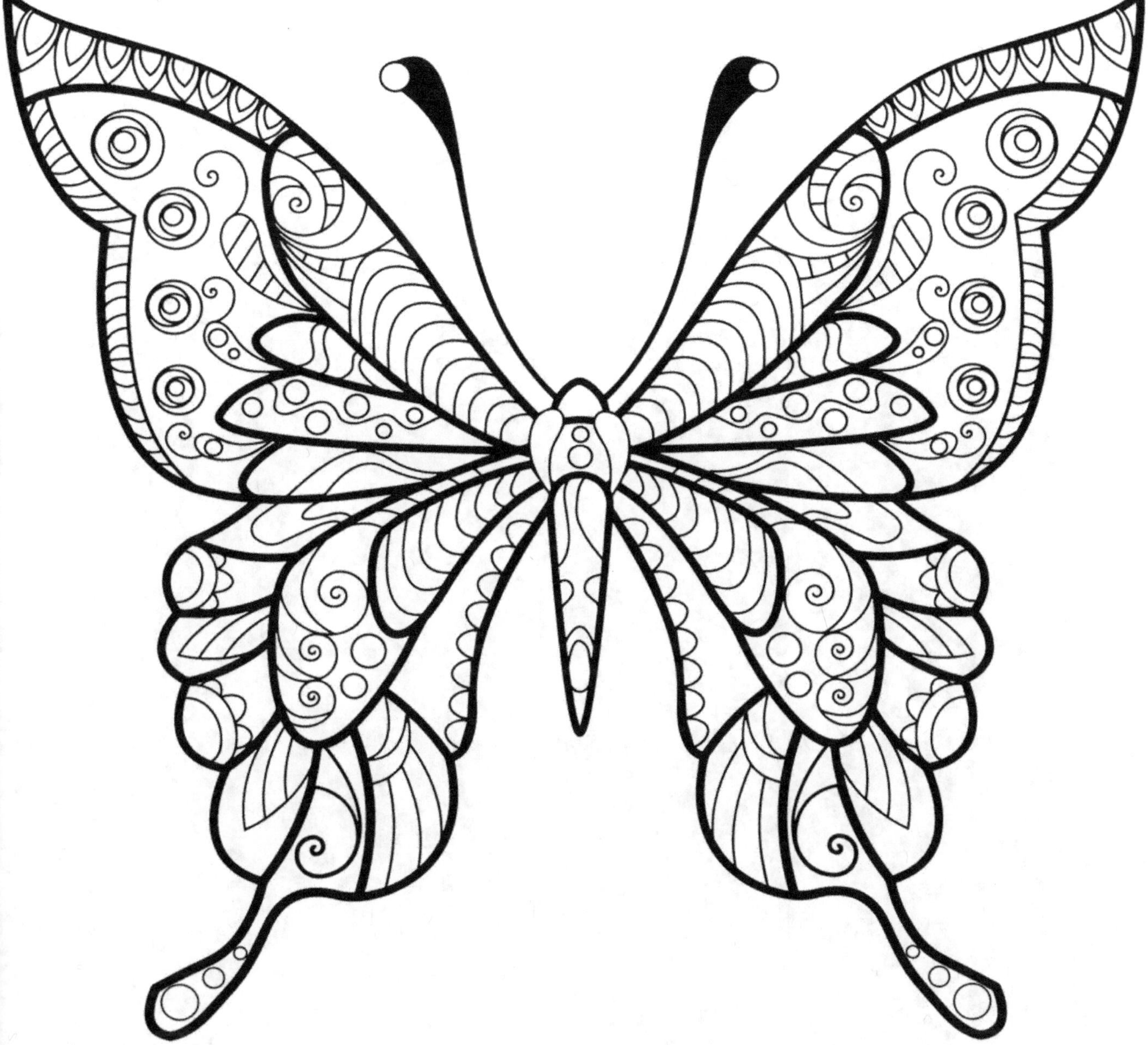

Butterfly Coloring Pages

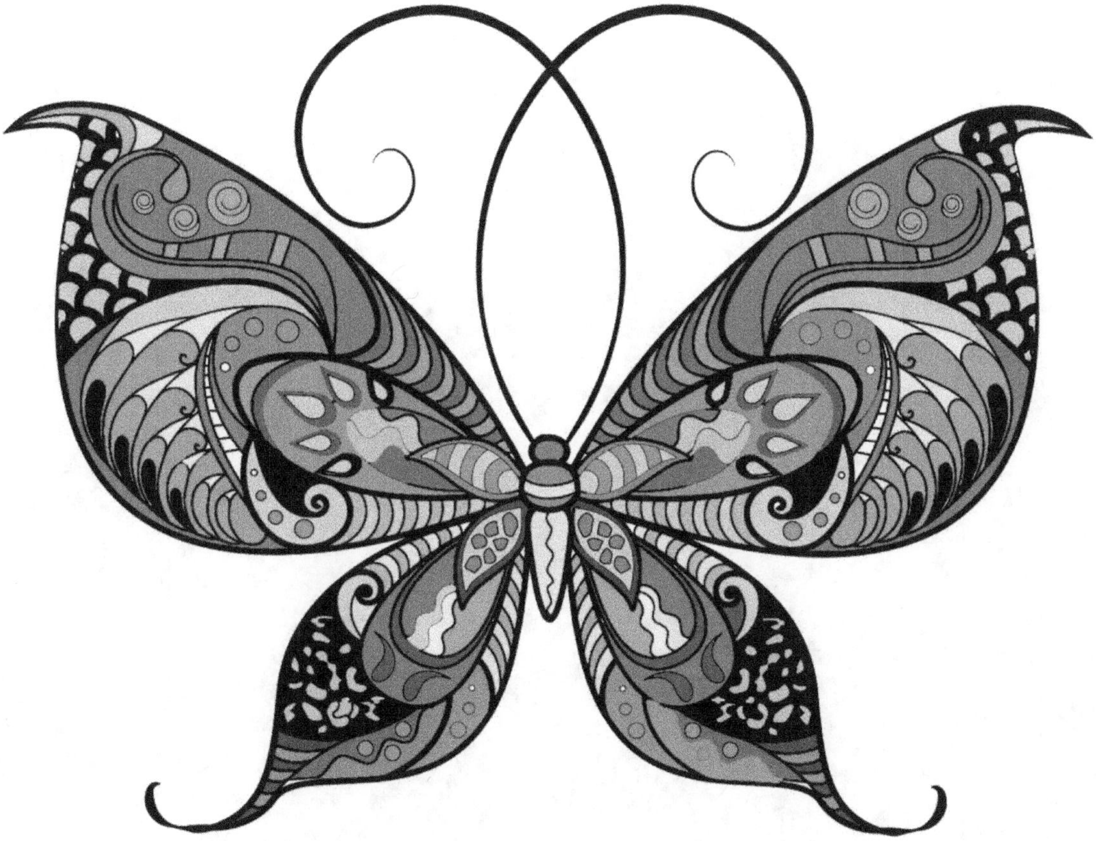

www.ingramcontent.com/pod-product-compliance
Lightning Source LLC
Chambersburg PA
CBHW081420220526
45467CB00009B/2766